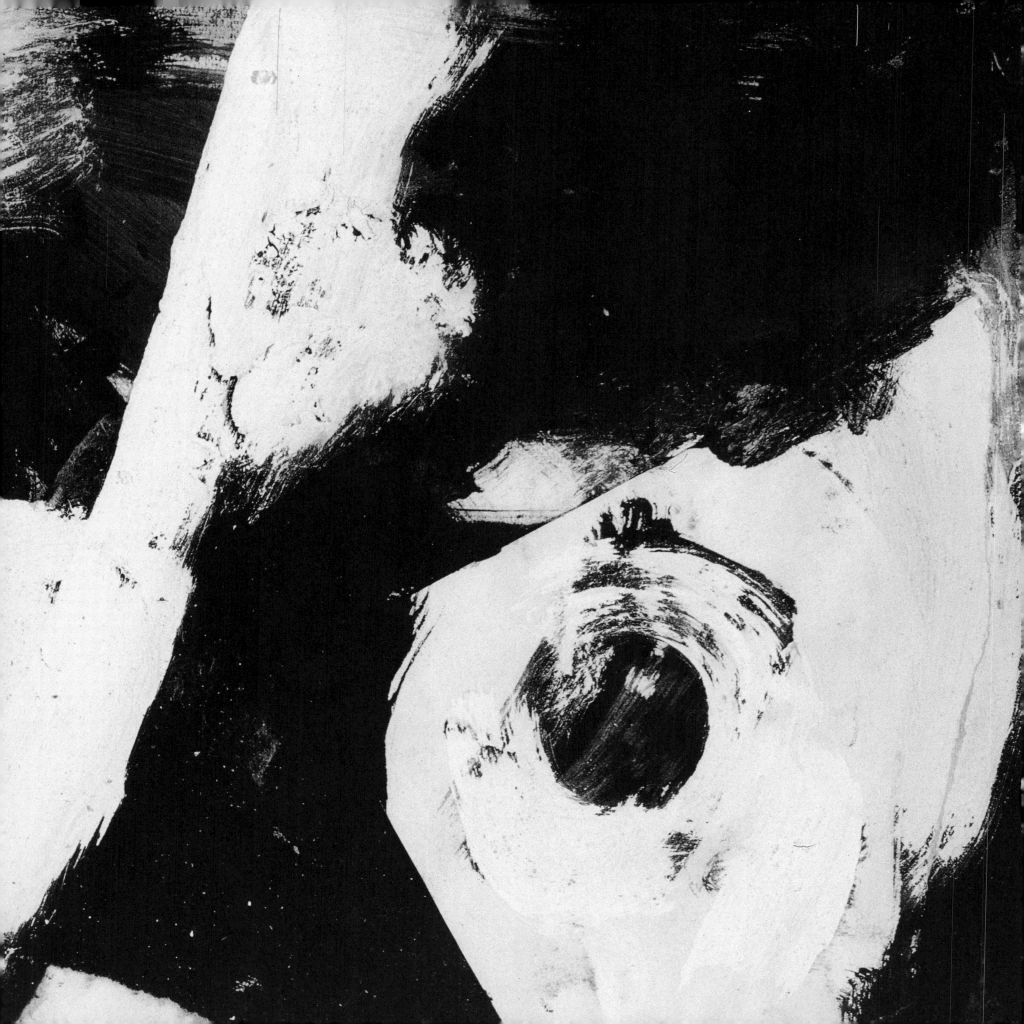

rediscovering

william**freed**

William Freed in his Provincetown studio, 1980s

W ho would have thought that the adventure into Freed's creative eye would become this massive output of pictorial surprises? Most of the paintings and works on paper I remembered, but a large number of works I did not. Because Bill liked to review his work, he would add or change the composition which resulted in a new pictorial image. He thought of his work as "alive" and "never finished."

In preparing for his show, I felt I was "rediscovering" William Freed, an artist I knew most of his creative life. The works being shown at both CMFA (Cape Museum and Fine Art) and PAAM (Provincetown Art Association and Museum) represent a fraction of his productivity.

Freed was not dogmatic or formalistic; on the contrary he had an analytical and dialectical mind and he sought pictorial expression through cubism, planes, colored shapes, and forms — at times superimposing plastically the line over the picture plane. He was searching for a pictorial expression that would relate to his response to nature.

The Freed retrospectives had their origins at Berta Walker's cocktail party in the fall of 2000 where I met Robert Warshaw, Trustee of the Hofmann Foundation. From the moment we began to talk, the seeds were planted. We approached Gregory Harper, who was the Director of CMFA, at that time. Greg's enthusiasm and interest in Freed's work secured a slot for a one person exhibition. As the project details became a reality, the Provincetown Art Association and Museum was included as an exhibition venue because of Freed's long standing relationship with PAAM and the galleries in Provincetown. Don Knaub, current Director of CMFA, and Christine McCarthy, Director of PAAM, deserve special thanks for aiding and continuing a project that was conceived prior to their arrival on the Cape. This dual undertaking led to three more exhibition venues — at the Cherrystone Gallery in Wellfleet, the Acme Fine Art in Boston, and the Beauregard Gallery in Rumson, NJ. Between 2003 and 2004 there will be a total of five Freed exhibitions.

What appeared to be a routine selection of Bill's work became a mammoth undertaking as we looked through oils, watercolors, drawings, works on paper, collages, and some sculpture. It all came together after I received assistance from the following — Robert Henry for works on paper and James Bennette and David Cowan for oils.

Bill was once asked if he enjoyed being an artist. His reply was "NO — because in the act of creation I struggle with how best to express myself. Frankly, the act of creating is often frustrating and emotionally draining whereas the viewer enjoys the finished work and the collector has the pleasure of owning a work of art." Freed added, "I would have preferred to have been a collector. Instead I became an artist."

Enjoy!
Lillian Orlowsky, 2003

Freed's humble manner didn't give a clue to the power of his presence in New York and Provincetown. He had been a mainstay of Hofmann's inner circle of friends and former students ever since 1939. For over fifty years his painting enlivened exhibitions involving the WPA, the American Abstract Artists, the second generation of Abstract Expressionists, the artists of the Tenth Street scene, Provincetown painters, and former Hofmann students.

The more I see of the great range of his work — from loosely brushed ink to interlocking penciled planes to rich veins of oil — the more I am impressed by the lyricism of his color. His planes rotate like a mobile, giving weight to the whimsical. Using gravity to attain flight makes sense enough, but the mercurial quality of Freed's trajectories and the resonance of his floating forms alter our kinetic sensibility.

Tina Dickey
Editor, Hans Hofmann Catalogue Raisonné

Lillian Orlowsky & William Freed in Provincetown, 1952

william freed

a disciplined passion for art

by Myrna Harrison

William Freed called himself an "Abstract Realist." These two words not only describe the complexity of the aesthetic of his late paintings, but also the range of his work from the early twentieth century when he did small, meticulously rendered academic drawings of the nude at the Educational Alliance until the end of the century when he exhibited large abstract brilliantly colored oil paintings in a Retrospective at the Provincetown Art Association and Museum in 1981. Although Freed's earliest work embraces academic realism and his last work abstraction, he did not believe that abstraction was better than realism, but rather that abstraction and realism were two equal approaches to seeing and understanding the external world. For him abstraction was one way to portray the subject in front of him; realism was another.

The current retrospectives at the Provincetown Art Association and Museum and the Cape Museum of Fine Art reveal the rich variety of Freed's work. The exhibitions are a fitting tribute to an artist whose vision helped to create and embody the major art movements of the twentieth century.

William Freed was born in 1902 in the Polish town of Przasnysz, about fifty-five miles north of Warsaw. He lived in the poverty-stricken Orthodox Jewish section of the town with his father, mother, grandmother, sister, two brothers — one an older half-brother — in a one-room, thatched-roof house without running water or electricity. When Freed was thirteen his father, a butcher, died. He remembered his father with little affection, describing him as "a very tough man" who beat him with a belt. But he was very fond of his mother who insisted on her children learning to read and write and sent them to the school taught by the local rabbi. The rabbi was a strict, narrow disciplinarian who beat the students if they

asked questions. Freed who always asked questions received many beatings. Despite the poverty and beatings, however, he did not remember his childhood with bitterness. Among his early paintings are numerous sympathetic portrayals of scenes from his childhood — of yoked water-carriers, of a wedding procession led by a rabbi and a violinist, and of himself being spanked by the rabbi.

Freed's early interest in drawing and painting is reflected in two childhood memories. The first was from the first world war, when some of Kaiser Wilhelm's soldiers were billeted in the Freed house. One, the watchman, stayed up all night drawing pictures of the towns he had stayed in. Freed later told Hans Hofmann about the German soldier who drew all night. Hofmann laughed and said, "Ah, the German Kaiser is responsible for your drawings." The second memory was of his fascination with the colorful Christian religious paintings for sale in the local marketplace. He wanted to study the images. But the orthodox Jewish community he grew up in believed he would be struck blind if he looked at them. The young Freed found a typically clever solution. He looked with one eye closed so that if God struck him, he could still see with one eye.

In 1922 William Freed emigrated to the United States, settling in New York City on the Lower East Side. After several temporary construction jobs, he got a job in a cabinet making shop where he developed a skill that he enjoyed and worked at for the rest of his life

Freed began his study of art at the Educational Alliance, a settlement house on the Lower East Side designed to help recent immigrants learn the language and customs of their new country. Freed enrolled at the Alliance to learn English, but one evening while wandering through the halls, he saw a drawing class and was intrigued. He decided that he would learn English on his own and study art at the Alliance He started with an etching class, then briefly studied sculpture with Chaim Gross, and finally chose a drawing class. His instructors at the Alliance were Abbo Ostrowsky and Auerbach Levy. In 1929 after briefly enrolling in the Art Students League where he studied with Homer Boss and Richard Lahey, Freed returned to the Alliance. He later said that he got the same things free at the Alliance that he had to pay for at the League.

Becky Freed (left), Freed's sister-in-law & her brother, Freed, his aunt, and Becky's son Isidore at Freed's father's grave site in Poland, 1916

From the beginning William Freed's involvement with art was passionate and disciplined. After working long hours as a cabinet maker, he spent his evenings painting and drawing at the Alliance, his Saturdays attending galleries, and his Sundays painting portraits of models he hired from the Lower East Side or doing plein air paintings of the city's docks and parks. He quickly progressed from a beginner with little or no experience with drawing, to a monitor and then to a respected artist whose drawings and paintings were praised by instructors and students alike.

1928 was an important year in Freed's life. In that year he became a citizen of the United States and for the first time exhibited one of his paintings in an art exhibit. He was twenty-six years old. Citizenship signaled his decision to become part of his new country. Exhibiting a landscape at the Society of Independent Artists was a public statement of his determination to become a professional artist.

Unlike most students and teachers at the Alliance and League, Freed deeply respected the work of Manet, Cezanne, Van Gogh, Rouault and Soutine, modern European painters who were then largely ignored or rejected in the United States. These painters, particularly Cezanne, would have a lifelong influence on his work. He also frequented the Art Room of the New York Public Library to study the works of earlier masters like Rembrandt, Michelangelo, Vermeer and Titian. At first it was difficult for Freed to get the books he wanted because he didn't know how to use the card catalog and he was very shy — as he was throughout his life, except with close friends. Freed solved the problem of getting the

books he wanted in a creative way. He realized there was another person in the room who had similar tastes in art books so when this patron returned his books to the desk, Freed would ask for them. The librarian soon realized what was happening and would take the books returned by the first patron directly to Freed. That first patron was Mark Rothko.

Sometime in 1932 or 33, Freed met Lillian Orlowsky, whom he would later marry. When Orlowsky told him that she was interested in the arts, Freed suggested that she attend the Educational Alliance. Orlowsky later said that Freed who had been at the Alliance for ten years "...came in like the master. He did what I thought to be marvelous drawings. The instructor, Ostrowsky, had a great deal of respect for him and his work. All the students did. I think he came there, at the time I was there, just as a visiting artist who had no place to work."

During the Depression, the Federal Art Project (FAP), part of the Work Project Administration (WPA), stimulated American art by paying artists for their work and bringing artists together who might not otherwise have known each other. William Freed worked for the Federal Art Project from 1937 to 1941 in the divisions of Art Education and Mural Painting. As part of the Art Education Division, he returned to the Educational Alliance as an instructor. As a member of the Mural Division, he worked initially as an assistant to his friend Louis Schanker on a tempera on canvas mural for the New York City radio station WNYC. He then worked as an assistant to George McNeil, who became a lifelong friend and with whom he would share a studio in the village and later in Provincetown, MA. The long lines that developed as artists waited to pick up their checks of $23.86 a week led to vibrant discussions about art. William Freed and Lillian Orlowsky, who also worked on the Federal Art Project, participated in these discussions along with Jackson Pollock, Philip Guston, Lee Krasner, Arshile Gorky and many others.

William Freed (left) and James Gahagan preparing the
Hans Hofmann mosaic mural at 711 Third Avenue

Freed working in his studio in Provincetown, 1960

In the late thirties, William Freed and Lillian Orlowsky heard about Hans Hofmann, the German painter whose cubist-inspired work was derided by many New York artists. Orlowsky was the first to try Hofmann's school. She told Freed how exciting it was and urged him to see for himself. He said he would try a class with Hofmann and maybe stay a month. Freed often told the story about his first experience drawing from the nude in the Hofmann class. He drew the kind of small, isolated on the paper, perfectly detailed academic study of a nude that he had learned to draw from Ostrowsky at the Educational Alliance. Hofmann looked at Freed's drawing and made a disparaging comment. Freed was stunned. But he was fascinated with the detailed criticism Hofmann gave to every student and with Hofmann's own drawings, sometimes done over the student's drawing, sometimes done in small boxes he outlined in charcoal at the top of the student's drawing. Freed stayed to study with Hofmann for the next ten years — until 1947.

World War II started in Europe in 1939 and came to the United States in 1941 with the bombing of Pearl Harbor. In 1942 William Freed, a citizen for fourteen years, was drafted but declared 4F for health reasons. From 1941 to 1945, he worked in the Brooklyn Navy Yard building ships. Work on the ships was hard, dangerous and chaotic and when he came home he would not talk about what had happened that day.

In 1942, ten years after they first met, William Freed and Lillian Orlowsky were married. A year later, they began to look for an art community outside New York City where they could paint during the summers. In 1944 they settled in Provincetown, MA, where Hans Hofmann had set up a summer school. Their second year in

Provincetown they rented two studios in the Day's Lumber Yard. One studio Freed shared with George McNeil; the other studio was Lillian Orlowsky's and their living quarters. Over the years many artists rented studios in the complex, including Jan Muller, Robert Motherwell, Helen Frankenthaler, Jimmy Gahagan and Myron Stout. Hans

Hofmann also rented there, but lived elsewhere The artists who rented at the Lumberyard formed close bonds, frequently visiting each other's studios. The Provincetown Art Association and Museum recognized the importance of these relationships in their 1980 exhibition "The Lumberyard Painters." The Day's Lumber Yard Studios survive today as the home of the Fine Arts Work Center.

Each year in early May when William Freed and Lillian Orlowsky returned to Provincetown from New York, Freed set up three still lifes in his studio, which he painted from until the fall when he left The beauty and simplicity of Freed's still life set ups were well known. Sometimes after Freed had left for the winter, Hans Hofmann would come into Freed's studio and paint from them. Hofmann's Orchestral Dominance series (1954) was painted from one of Freed's still life set ups.

With the end of the war in 1945 the Hans Hofmann School of Fine Art in Provincetown flooded with students, many of them veterans, who came to study with the teacher who knew Picasso and drew his lineage from the cubists. Provincetown became the focal point for abstract and abstract expressionist art. It hummed with artists, art students, galleries, critics, and art conversation. William Freed and Lillian Orlowsky were part of the ferment — showing in the galleries, discussing art and its meaning, attending openings, participating in forums at the Provincetown Art Association and Museum.

The art ferment that characterized Provincetown in the summer characterized New York City in the winter, bringing new galleries to show the new art — many of them cooperatives on and around Tenth Street. In 1954 William Freed was one of the founding artists of the cooperative James Gallery on East 12th Street. Among the other founding artists were James Gahagan, James Billmyer, Charles Littler, Earl Pierce and Robert Henry.

Building Freed's studio and home in Provincetown
(left to right) WIlliam Freed, Lillian Orlowsky, James Gahagan and Myrna Harrison, 1960

Freed working in his studio, ca 1960

During the six years the gallery existed (1956-1962), William Freed had yearly solo exhibitions and participated in numerous group shows with artists such as Louise Nevelson, Robert Motherwell, Lee Krasner, Louise Bourgeois, Hans Hofmann and Adolph Gottlieb. In 1956 Hans Hofmann asked William Freed to be part of a four person team working on the cartoons for an abstract mosaic mural that Hofmann had been commissioned to design for a new office building at 711 Third Avenue in New York City. The other members of the team were James Gahagan, Max Spoerri, and Robert Fisher, all former Hofmann students. The mural was a 1,200 square foot mosaic designed to wrap around the elevator core and, in the words of the builders William Kaufman and Jack D. Weiler, to "vitalize the lobby and infuse it with the sense of the life that throbs so strongly all about us on Manhattan Island."

After fourteen summers renting at the Days' Lumberyard Studios in Provincetown, in 1958 William Freed and Lillian Orlowsky bought a lot on Brewster Street and began building their own studios and living space. Freed designed and built the studios from the ground up and then using his cabinet making skills designed and built the furniture that went into them. If people asked Freed when the studios would be finished, he answered, "They will never be finished, just like my paintings."

Whether he was in Provincetown or New York, William Freed led a passionate but disciplined art life. In New York he rose early to paint in his studio before going to work. Evenings he read about art or listened to music; on weekend nights he attended concerts or dined with friends. Saturdays he visited galleries and museums, where he saw the work of Picasso, Matisse, and Leger among others. In Provincetown his daily routine was to have a simple breakfast, followed by a morning painting in his studio, a simple lunch and an afternoon painting. After dinner, he sometimes returned to his studio, sometimes visited with other artists. In the late afternoon he and Lillian often went to one of the fresh water ponds in Wellfleet. William Freed's disciplined passion for art enabled him to produce not only hundreds of remarkable oil paintings, but also many works on paper. From the 1950's to the 1980's, he had twenty-two solo exhibitions and showed in more than 40 invitational and juried group shows throughout the United States and Europe

In 1976 William Freed suffered a stroke that interfered with his speaking, but not with his ability to see or paint. He recovered his ability to speak, but as a result of the stroke he developed

Parkinson's Disease which made it difficult for him to hold brushes. Despite this he continued his daily painting routine both in Provincetown and New York, completing the largest paintings of his career, some more than five feet high.

William Freed died in New York City of coronary shock following dental surgery in 1984. Shortly before his death he had received a grant from the Adolph and Esther Gottlieb Foundation. A month after his death, the Ingber Gallery in New York City opened a memorial exhibition of large oil paintings most of which had been completed within the year.

William Freed's disciplined passion for art created a large luminous body of work that reflects the major art currents of the twentieth century. From his early academic realist works to his late abstract and semi-abstract still lifes, his work is characterized by its expressionist intensity, thoughtful composition and vibrant color. The current retrospective exhibitions at the Cape Museum of Art of Fine Art in Dennis and the Provincetown Art Association and Museum in Provincetown reveal the extraordinary range of this fine painter's work.

Freed on St. Marks Place, New York, 1938

Peddlers

1939 Oil on canvas
24 x 30 inches

Facing page
Peddlers, *detail*

Man in Bowler

1929 Oil on canvas
20 x 28 inches

Portrait of Man & Woman

1923 Oil on canvas
26¼ x 18¼ inches

Morning, East Second Street

early 1930's Oil on canvas
30 x 40 inches

Facing page
Coney Island Boatyard

early 1930's Oil on canvas
28 x 24 inches

Still Life of Broom

late 1940's Oil on canvas

26 x 20 inches

Still Life of Utensils

late 1940's Oil on canvas
30 x 24 inches

Black & White Still Life

1939 Oil on canvas
19 x 17 inches

Facing page

Black Chair & Bottle

1959 Oil on canvas
44 x 36 inches

Still Life of Fruit & Bottle

1963 Oil on canvas

32 x 27 inches

Still Life of Coffee Pots

early 1970's Oil on canvas
18 x 24 inches

Facing page

Purple Background & Reds

1981 Oil on canvas
40 x 32 inches

Still Life & Chair

1984 Oil on plywood
35 x 18 inches

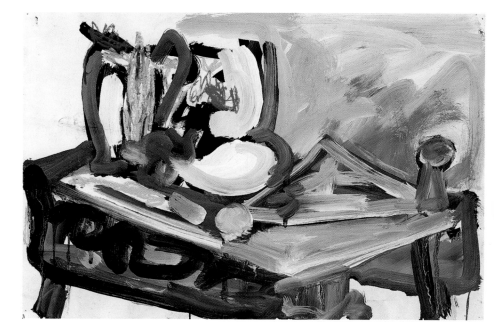

Still life
1961 Tempera on paper
24 x 18 inches

Still life
1968 Tempera & crayon paper
18 x 24 inches

Still life
1960's Tempera on paper
24 x 18 inches

Still life
1968 Tempera & crayon paper
16 x 24 inches

Jars on Shapes

1980 Oil on canvas
50 x 32 inches

Still life

1968 Crayon & tempera on paper
24 x 18 inches

Still life

1960 Ink & tempera on paper
24 x 18 inches

william freed

poetic craftsman — painter

by Ronald Andrew Kuchta
New York, 2003

I remember Bill Freed well, as modest in stature and manner but imposing as a man both insistently inquisitive and doggedly productive throughout his life. He was a respected painter who regularly attended openings at the Chrysler Museum in Provincetown along with his wife, the artist Lillian Orlowsky. Occasionally they'd invite me to dinner at the house Bill built on Brewster Street, the lane where many artists such as Myron Stout and Seong Moy had studios. Its interior was always filled with paintings — his and Lillian's — and while we dined, I was poignantly aware of the tremendous aesthetic efforts expended on the numerous canvases surrounding me. At that time I was curator of the Chrysler Museum; in those heady days — the boom years of the sixties — our conversations at dinner often touched on Mr. Chrysler's latest collecting pursuits — from the important Picassos and Matisses he had shown in his museum to the debatable works from the aptly titled "Controversial Century" show of 1962, which some critics had dismissed as spurious. Provincetown was inundated with artists and galleries of exceptional quality in the sixties; Tirca Karlis, OK Harris, HCE, the Sun, Esther Stuttman, Virginia Zabriskie, Paul Kessler, 256 Cooperative, and the East End were all galleries where I'd run into Bill and Lillian at numerous openings.

I admired Freed's prodigious and conscientious production of art and his homage to Hans Hofmann, whom my mentor and employer Walter P. Chrysler Jr. considered the greatest living painter in America.

Years later, in the late seventies, as Director of the Everson Museum of Art in Syracuse, New York, I escorted the famous formalist critic Clement Greenberg through the exhibition I had curated called "Provincetown Painters" which surveyed over 70 years of artistic production. The exhibition contained a comprehensive view of American art, including the works of many painters Greenberg especially thought well of, like Hans Hofmann and his numerous former students. He included a work by Bill Freed titled *Symphonics* of 1942. This painting is an abstraction exemplifying the influence of cubism about which Greenberg glowingly wrote, "Cubism remains the greatest phenomenon, the epoch making feat of twentieth century art, a style that has changed and determined the complexion of Western art as radically as Renaissance naturalism once did." He called cubism "the only vital style of our time."

Freed was an immigrant as were many of the eventually well known painters of his generation whom he knew including Mark Rothko, Adolf Gottlieb, and Willem de Kooning. Freed became a student of Hans Hofmann after studying at the Educational Alliance and the Art Students League in New York.

Freed's earliest paintings, most of them undated, from the 1920s and into the 30s are influenced by Cezanne whom Freed admitted to always admiring. The local landscapes are close in feeling to Rouault whose work I don't believe he knew at that time. The vertical and diagonally bent structures of the trees in these early colorful compositions and the more block-like cubistic rocks in the landscapes prefigure perhaps Freed's inclination to draw parallel compositions in his later abstractions.

Quite distinct are Freed's paintings of the late 20s and early 30s (a chronology I assume from the rather vague dating of his pictures) include works depicting figurative scenes with obvious social narratives as is the case in "Polish Village Scene," "Morning on Orchard Street" and "Sleeping Truck Man" of 1930. In these canvases Freed interprets his childhood memories of Poland and of the lower east side of New York City during the economic depression as did many of his contemporaries who later turned to abstraction including his friends Rothko and Gottlieb. In his recent book, *American Expressionism: Art and Social Change 1920-1930*, Bram Dijkstra suggests that many of the artists of this period turned away from politically inspired or social commentary art in the 40s and 50s to disengage from leftist-leaning artists like William Gropper who was later incriminated by rightist political factions. Another argument for artists such as Freed turning from figurative realism or socially conscious subject matter to abstraction was the change in patronage away from government support through the WPA, for instance (Freed was with the mural division of the WPA from 1937 to 1941), to the private support of galleries, individual collectors or corporations whose tastes tended toward the abstract and much less towards the socially conscious themes of the realists or expressionists of the pre-World War II era.

Still life
1960's Crayon on paper
24 x 18 inches

The modern French art movement, in particular the work of Picasso, was of great interest to Freed during the late 30s and early 40s. Figurative works such as "Unsettled" (a cubist man beating another man), "Peddlers" of 1939 (page 10-11) and "Bearded Cellist" took on a more cubist perspective.

By 1942, in another untitled work, Freed created a complex composition of interlocking planes with almost no drawing. Small figures are practically consumed by an overwhelming environment of colorful, angular blocks, foreboding perhaps. The complete disappearance of human figures from Freed's paintings is apparent until their rare inclusion, much abstracted, in the late fifties.

From the late forties on, the abstract still-life dominates Freed's oeuvre. Rhythmic, disciplined and structured with line and color, Freed painted from nature, his own sensibility and questioning nature investigating each subject and interpreting each still-life or scene in a studied succession of efforts to achieve an aesthetic harmony. Vertical lines complemented with diagonals, often creating a triangular drawing in many compositions, characterize many of Freed's most original works of this period. In these painted lines, shapes and forms, rhythmic or jagged, Freed's unique signature and expression were cogently revealed.

In the late 50s and early 60s Freed's painting developed into a personal expression and his relationship with color dictated purely non-objective compositions. These examples of non-objectivity are exceptional, however, and Freed's fascination with nature and drawing took hold again as he invariably returned to still-life enlivened once again by his strong sense of rhythm and color.

Again during the late 50s and early 60s in paintings such as "Provincetown by the Sea" and "Green Light" a continued interest in the suggested figure is revealed in shimmering landscapes and rather poetic Milton Avery-like approaches to the seashore subject matter surrounding his Cape Cod studio. Later paintings, such as "White Floating Forms" of 1981 return to less objective abstractions with color and line dominating a roughly painted surface. Possibly a still-life yet ambiguously "floating" massive shapes intersect and inscribe with graphic, meandering lines, the calligraphic signature again revealing the artist's methodical, investigating mind.

Humble and quizzical, Freed was a cabinet maker by profession whose respect for craftsmanship is evident in his paintings. He would, I'm told, often sketch or paint as many as twenty or thirty works of the same subject challenging himself, I suppose, to "get it right," as he often described the process. Of drawing he is said to have indicated that before studying with Hans Hofmann "he didn't know what he was doing." Yet after turning to abstraction, Freed conscientiously pursued his own concepts and, I believe, created a large, distinctive body of work. His reputation may have suffered a bit because of his long association with Hofmann, as, I think, another friend of mine, Françoise Gilot's work is often unfairly compared to Picasso's because of her close personal relationship with him. But while Freed undoubtedly absorbed much of Hofmann's criticism and teachings, his inimitable sense of structural composition, color and the calligraphic use of line to trace the circuitous channels of his own imagination make his treatment of his canvases unique and his poetic efforts to create high-quality pictures all the more original.

Extremely acute and articulate, Freed's written statement about his own work is worth quoting here. "I want to paint the visible as well as the invisible," Freed wrote for the Ingber Gallery for his one-person exhibition in 1984: "I take my inspiration from nature. Art cannot be made dogma, therefore I do not repeat myself; each painting represents a unique experience. I anticipate struggle and disappointment but approach my canvas with appetite and enthusiasm. My idea is to create new forms and color, away from the prismatic, more towards the psychological which might introduce a unique expression."

Thus, Freed the poetic painter-craftsman aspired to achieve his goal of creating works that bear quiet penetration to delight our eyes with color and form as well as to challenge our mentalities.

Figure Drawing
1940's Ink on paper
10 x 8 inches

Cubist Stage Set

late 1930's Oil on canvas
28 x 36 inches

Cubist Figure Drawing

1937 Charcoal on paper
25 x 19 inches

Figures Under Tree

late 1930's Oil on canvas
15 x 19 inches

Facing page

Figures Under Tree, *detail*

Pinks, Greens & Orange

early 1940's Oil on masonite
29¾ x 24 inches

Blues, Orange & Peach

early 1940's Oil on canvas
36 x 28 inches

Still Life of Fruit & Bottle

1948 Oil on canvas
32 x 27 inches

Facing page

Purple Shapes

1960's Oil on canvas
46 x 42 inches

Blues & Oranges

1980's Oil on canvas
30 x 24 inches

Greens & Blacks

late 1940's Oil on canvas
42 x 32 inches

Previous page
Primary Geometric

1978 Oil on canvas
26 x 50 inches

Yellow & Red Diamond Shape

late 1970'S Oil on canvas
36 x 22 inches

Easel on Red Background

1970's Oil on canvas
30 x 28 inches

Blue, Green & Orange

1954 Oil on canvas
41½ x 32 inches

Yellow, Orange & Black

1958 Oil on canvas
42 x 32 inches

Peach Background & Eye

1950's Oil on canvas
25 x 35 inches

After The Sunset

early 1950's Oil on masonite
24 x 20 inches

Red Shapes

1960's Oil on canvas
36 x 28 inches

The Nightly Blues

1958 Oil on board
20 x 25 inches

Blue Background, Red & Pinks

1960 Oil on canvas
50 x 30 inches

White Oval   *(cover detail)*

1970's Oil on canvas
31 x 37 inches

Red Horizon

1967 Oil on canvas
50 x 42 inches

biographical notes

1902 Born, July 26, Poland
1922 Arrives in U.S.A.
1924 Educational Alliance Art School, New York;
Abbo Ostrowsky, Auerbach Levy, instructors.
1928 U.S. citizen
1929 Art Student's League, Homer Boss and
Richard Lahey, instructors.
1937-41 WPA teachers and mural division, assistant to
Louis Schanker, executed mural for
radio station WNYC.
Also assisted George McNeil.
1937-47 Hans Hofmann School of Fine Art, W. 9th St. and
8th St. New York, NY
1941-45 Worked in Brooklyn Navy Yard, New York, NY
1942 Married Lillian Orlowsky, artist
1944 First summer in Provincetown, MA
1945-60 Days Studio
1956 One of the founders of the James Gallery, 70 E.
12th St., New York, NY
1956 Assisted Hans Hofmann on mural for Kaufman
Building, 711 3rd Ave., New York, NY
1960-63 Built own studio in Provincetown, MA

one-person exhibitions

1955-62 James gallery, six one-man shows, New York, NY
1957-60 H C E Gallery, Provincetown, MA
1960 Esther Stuttman Gallery, Provincetown, MA
New Arts Gallery, Atlanta, GA
1962 Esther Stuttman Gallery, New York, NY
1965 Esther Stuttman Gallery, Washington, D.C.
1967 Artisan Gallery, Brunswick, ME
1976-80 Tirca Karlis Gallery, Provincetown, MA
1979 Goddard College, Plainfield, VT
1980 Lenore Ross Gallery, Provincetown, MA
1981 *In Retrospect*, PAAM, Provincetown, MA
2000 Tours, France
2004 Acme Fine Art, Boston, MA

selected group shows

1928 Society of Independent Artists, New York, NY
1936 Municipal Art Week, New York, NY
1936-67 A C A Gallery, New York, NY
1937-40 Federal Art Project Gallery, New York, NY
1941 *39th Annual Philadelphia Water-color and Print*,
Philadelphia, PA
1946-80 PAAM, Provincetown, MA
1949 Gallery 49, Provincetown, MA
1952 Riverside Museum, *Kaufman Gallery*, YMHA
1953-67 H C E Gallery, Provincetown, MA
1954 *Abbo Ostrowsky Collection*, Jewish Museum
Riverside Museum, *Kaufman Gallery*, YMHA
1954-62 James Gallery, New York, NY
1956 Sun Gallery, Provincetown, MA
Riverside Museum, *Kaufman Gallery*, YMHA
Audubon Society, New York, NY
1956-63 Museum of Modern Art Lending Library
1958 Gallery 256, Provincetown, MA
Riverside Museum, *Kaufman Gallery*, YMHA
Audubon Society, New York, NY
Burluik Gallery, New York, NY
Worcester Museum, Worcester, MA
1958-59 Boston Arts Festival, Boston, MA
1959 Whitney Museum of American Arts, New York, NY
Riverside Museum, *Kaufman Gallery*, YMHA
Audubon Society, New York, NY
American Abstract Artist, Riverside Museum, NY
deCordova and Dana Museum and Park,
Lincoln, MA

1959-60 Whitney Museum of American Art, *Art U.S.A.*
1960 New York University Art Collection exhibit
Kresge Art Gallery, Michigan State University,
Lansing, MI
1962 Corcoran Gallery, Washington, D.C.
1963-65 *Hofmann and His Students*, Museum of Modern
Art Traveling exhibition
1964 Museum of Modern Art Lending Library
1965 Golden Anniversary of PAAM, MA
1967 Esther Stuttman Gallery, Washington, D.C.
1970 Chrysler Museum of Art, Provincetown, MA
First Major New England Show of the 70's, Boston
Arts Center, Boston, MA
1971 *Free Abstract Form of the 50's*, Whitney Museum
of American Art, New York, NY
Provincetown 3rd Invitational Show
Chrysler Museum of Art, Provincetown, MA
1977 WPA, *Then and Now*, Parsons School of Design,
New York, NY
1978 *Provincetown Painters, 1890's-1970's*, Everson
Museum, Syracuse, NY
10th Street in 1977, Landmark Gallery
CO-OPS of 10th St., Ward-Nasse Gallery
1980 *Hans Hofmann as a Teacher*, drawn from the collec-
tions of the Metropolitan Museum of Art
and the PAAM
1981 In Retrospect, PAAM, Provincetown, MA
Adelphi University, Garden City, New York
1999 *Forum 49 Revisited*, PAAM, MA
2000 Copenhagen, Denmark
2001 Cape Museum of Fine Arts, Dennis, MA
2002 Acme Fine Art, Boston, MA
2003 Acme Fine Art, Boston, MA
Beauregard Gallery, Rumson, NJ
Cherrystone Gallery, Wellfleet, MA
Hans Hofmann and His Students, PAAM, MA
Artists from the Sun Gallery, PAAM, MA
2004 Acme Fine Art, Boston, MA

reviews

1949 "*Art World Eyes Forum 49*", Roslyn Browne,
Advocate, Provincetown, MA, (July 7)
1951 New York Times, Stuart Preston, (August 19)
1952 "*This Week in the Art World*", Gene Brackley,
Boston Globe, Boston, MA. (August 24)
1956 Arts, James R. Mellow, (January)
Art News, Lawrence Cambell, (October)
Art, Elizabeth Goodman, (October)
Art, Howard Rachliffe, (October 18)
1957 New York Herald Tribune, Emily Genauer,
(December)
New York Times, Dorothy Ashton, (December 5)
1958 Art News, Irving Sandler, summer issue, (March)
Arts, James R. Mellow, (March)
Entertainment, "*Off Broadway*" Sylvia Lee,
(March 20)
Art News, James Schuyer, (July14)
Art, Ivan Karp, VIllage Voice, (December 17)
1959 Art News, Lillian Loongren, (February)
Herald Tribune, Carlyle Burrows, (February 22)
Arts, A. Ventura, (March)
Village Voice, Hillary Dunsterville, (December 17)
1962 The Evening Gazette, Frank Crotty, Worcester, MA,
(February 6)
New York Herald Tribune, newest pastime,
Emily Genauer, (March 18)
"*Off Broadway*", Sylvia Lee, (March 20)

taped interviews

1977 Dorothy Gees Seckler
1978 Cynthia Goodman for the Metropolitan
Museum of Art
1980 Advocate, summer issue, Art Guide Issue,
John Russel
Betty Bishop, transcript in progress

publications

1928 Catalogue, *Landscape Painting*, Society of
Independent Artists
1957 Palette Club of the Educational Alliance
1959 Arts Magazine (February)
1960-70 *Who's Who in American Art*
1962 New York Herald Tribune *Dance of Life*
1965 *Golden Anniversary Issue, Advocate*,
Provincetown, MA
Provincetown Art Association catalogue
1976 Special Arts Guide on New England Shows,
Provincetown, MA
Then and Now, WPA, New York
10th Street Co OP, catalogue
Artists at Work, One Place, Ben Brooks
1977 *Provincetown Painters* by Kuchta and Seckler,
Forum 49 exhibitors
1979 *Hofmann as Teacher and Artist*, Art Annual (April)
Provincetown Advocate (August)
1980 *Hofmann and His Students* interview by John
Russell in Advocate (August)
Hofmann as Teacher, Metropolitan Museum of Art
1981 *In Retrospect*, exhibition catalog, PAAM

awards

1957 1st Prize, Cape Cod Art Association, Hyannis, MA,
Jurors Karl Knaths, Myron Stout and
Mary Cecil Allen
1960 Longview Foundation Purchase Award
1967 Chapelbrook Foundation Grant
1976 Goddard College Annual Cash Award, Best in Show
1984 Adolph and Esther Gottlieb Foundation Grant

works in public collections

Cape Museum of Fine Arts, Dennis, MA
Chrysler Museum, Norfolk, VA
Illya Schor Foundation, New York, NY
Jewish Museum, New York, NY
Magnes Museum, San Francisco, CA
Metropolitan Museum of Art, New York, NY
New York University Art Collection, New York, NY
PAAM, Provincetown, MA
University of Texas, Austin, TX
Whitney Museum of American Art, New York, NY
Archives of the Smithsonian Institute, Washington, D.C
Rose Museum, Brandeis University, Waltham, MA
Jewish Museum of the West, Berkeley, CA

Repose
1957 Oil on canvas
42 x 32 inches.
The Whitney Museum of American Art, New York; purchase, with funds from an anonymous donor

My thanks to the Renate, Hans and Maria Hofmann Trust for making this project possible. I must single out Robert Warshaw, Patricia Gallagher and Mark Altschuler for their help.

And to the others who have helped: Gregory Harper, Donald Knaub, Christine McCarthy, Robert Henry, David Cowan, James Bennette, Sally Nerber, Kathy Donnelly, Angela and Richard Belski, Myrna Harrison, Ronald Kuchta, Claire Sprague, Hannah Alderfer, Betty Bishop, Tina Dickey, Chris Busa, Jim Yohe, Kristina Bird, Anthony Moore, Clement and Howcraft, The Staffs of CMFA and PAAM, Jean Lesser, Liz McLean, Madeline Amgott, Shirley Lothenberg, Fran Charbeneau, Laura Anderson and Wayne Petty, Debra, Paul Resika, Stephen D'Agostino.

This catalog was published on the occasion of the exhibition
Rediscovering William Freed

Oil paintings
September 6 – November 2, 2003
Opening reception September 26

Cape Museum of Fine Arts
60 Hope Lane, PO Box 2034,
Dennis, MA 02638
tel 508-385-4477

Works on paper
September 26 – November 2 2003
Opening reception September 27

Provincetown Art Association and Museum
760 Commercial Street
Provincetown, MA 02657
tel 508-487-4750

photography of artwork by Clements/Howcroft, Boston

photographers
page 2: Martin Green
   4&5: Maurice Bereza
      7: left: Jean Lesser; right: Sam May
      8: left: Sam May; right: Lillian Orlowsky
    22: Gloria Nardin
    55: Geoffrey Clements
 above: Paul Resika and William Freed at the Emmerich Gallery
            January 23, 1979; by Robert Del Tredici

Cover: White Oval (detail) 1970's Oil on canvas 37 x 31 inches
Endpapers: Figure Drawings (detail) Charcoal on paper 1960s
      18 x 24 inches

Foreword Lillian Orlowsky © 2003
Statement Tina Dickey © 2003
William Freed, A Disciplined Passion for Art
      Myrna Harrison © 2003
William Freed, Poetic Craftsmen – Painter
      Ronald Andrew Kuchta © 2003

Design by HHA design, Sarah & Hannah Alderfer
Printed by Paola Gribaudo, Turin Italy
Edition:5,000

ISBN: 0-9721979-1-5